Aglaonema

(Ag-lao-nema)

Krystal D. Moreland

In memory of my late grandmother

Mrs. Mary Lizzie Moreland

Thank you is the least I can say to you to show my appreciation for everything you have done for me.

Acknowledgements

To my Parents, Amari, and Mandy: I love you so much. Thank you for always being there and believing in me.

To Tamara: Thank you for being such a supportive cousin and for being such a warm spirit. You are beautiful, strong and appreciated.

To Jamaal and Talisa: You both have been amazing friends, holding down the cheer section. I love you both for being so supportive in this project.

To my Family and Friends: Thank you everything you've done whether it has been listening to me vent, giving advice, or just giving words of encouragement.

CONTENTS

Preface

I wrote this for people like me that have gone through the joy of relationships and the pain of heartbreak. I thought Aglaonema is a plant that manages to flourish despite being in a dimly lit setting. I thought *Aglaonema* would be a good title for this collection of poetry because it is about being able to love despite being put through the ringer by heartbreak after heartbreak.

As we all know love has never been easy, but it's truly worth it.

You can continue to grow in love after heartbreak. I have always been a firm believer that you should never dim the light within you just because everything around you has become dim.

Let your inner aglaonema unfold and don't let your past discourage your future.

Giving LOVE is like gambling,
you take your chances
and
if you're lucky enough to
win it's the most joyous feeling ever.

There's Something About You

As I sit here in the dark and think of you I
realize every feeling you've
ever had for me I strongly feel them for
you

Regardless of the mileage between us our
mind, body, and soul act as one
for this bond we share no one can break or
go beyond

You are my early morning, mid day, and
late night craving there's one thing for
sure
Whenever you need my affection I'm
always willing to give you more
More of my spirit I will give to you freely,
the words you speak always intrigue me.
Try as I might, I can't seem to get you off
my mind

so I just let my feelings for you flow
within the heart of this rhyme
It's 3 o'clock in the morning now and I
have nothing to do
but sit here in the dark and lovingly think
of you.
What is it about you? What is it that drives
me crazy?
I don't know but whatever it is has me
wanting to be your one and only lady.

Give Me A Minute To...

Give me a second to kiss your lips
I'll take another five to caress your soul with
poetic words of truth and thoughts of you

Spare me nine seconds for me to look into your eyes
and search for your powerful inner strength that I long for.
Ten seconds in your arms gives me such security that I call
you my soothing place from this ever so chaotic world
I'd take fifteen seconds to make wild crazy love with your
beautiful mind til the point to where we reach outrageous
heights of pleasure and passion that I once thought were unreachable.

Twenty seconds is all it'll take for me to
say how much my love for you
has grown and that I think of you every
awakening hour of my day

Baby I could give you a lifetime of
happiness if you just give me a minute to
show you.

Zeus

He is kind,

    strong,

        bright,

            handsome

He is every bit of the word man. If I ever needed saving he has the only pair of arms I'd feel safe in.

His kisses are filled with electric bolts of passion. He can make me love him all over again with the curvature of his mouth creating the most breathtaking smile.

He is stubborn,

temperamental,

secretive,

intense

He walks in authority and handles his business like none other. He always has a lot on his mind but he shares very little of what he's thinking. Maybe one day he will let me in one day.

He rarely gets a full night of sleep and whenever he's asked why he usually says that it's a lot going on. I wish I could help him when he's up fighting with his demons while the rest of the world is sleeping.

Tell Me How It Feels...

Tell me what it feels like to be touched by him in such a way it makes your spine tingle.

Tell me what it feels like to hear him say that he needs you and you're the only one that he's been thinking about.

Tell me what it feels like to have his scent lingering in your home.

Tell me what it feels like to lay your head on your pillow and reminisce about the many nights before that you could roll over and see his face.

Tell me what it feels like to be devoured by his passion.

Tell me what it feels like to hear him say he loves you and put confidence in saying that you are his and he is all yours.

Tell me what it feels like to put your trust in him because you know that he would never do anything to distort your trust. Tell me, just tell me what it feels like to be his fool.

When the Sun Rises...

What do we do when the sun rises and we
have to go our separate ways?
Do we forget about how we spent last
night in each others
arms doing a little "last minute work"?
All the while knowing you don't belong to
me....nor I to you.

Or
Do we let our night stay on our mind and
prepare for the next take over of
temptation?

But last night, oh my sweet darling that
night, we
created our own night to remember yet we
seem
to have forgotten about the love we have
at home.

What will they do when the sun sets and it's time for us to reunite?
Will they sit and wait by the phone until we call to let them
know it's gonna be another "late night at work" like we expect them to?

Or
Will they go out for a little rendezvous of their own and beat us to the house to be there to
greet us after we get home

when the sun rises?

LOVE is a shapeshifter.

Different Sides of the Field

I can't love you like I should because I
can't make my heart
feel what something that's nonexistent so
why waste
your time?

Why should I have you putting your all
into something
that will never be? It's unfair for you to
come 85 and I
only give you 15 yet for some reason you
continue to
stick it out and make it stretch like your
last five
dollar bill.

I don't understand it, why would you stay
with a

hopeless love and continue to be cheated
out of

most of what should be someone else's?
There is someone
out there who can treat better than I have
and better than
I probably ever would
In order for you to find her you have to let
me go.

Love Won't Let Me

Mama's fussing, Daddy's disappointed
whatever it is you do to me I never need it
but I continue to want it
I know you're no good and that I should
leave but what am I to do when
Love won't let me

We fuss all day and Fight all night
it seems that regardless of what I do for
you
I can never make it right
I know you're no good and that I should
leave but what am I to do when
Love won't let me

I can't understand why I put up with you
any sane person would leave but I can't
seem

to admit the fact that our relationship is
through

I know you're no good and that I should
leave but what am I to do when
Love won't let me

You could never make me happy
but I'm thankful to have found someone
that
can give his all to me
I know you're no good but I've found the
sense to leave I'm glad to say that
REAL LOVE HAS FOUND ME!

Submit Yourself

Submit yourself to me
give me all of you
tell me your true thoughts
tell me your fears
give me your pain so that
you will hurt no longer
come inside of my world and
I will submit myself to you
give you all of me
share the most personal of thoughts
the most pleasant of feelings
You and I are meant to be
I would love you like no other if
you submit yourself to me

Times Like These

Times like these I wish I could feel your touch
for your hands sends a sudden wave of pleasure every time we make hand to body contact

Times like these I wish I could taste the sweetness of your kiss which is closest experience to tasting candy rain I've ever had

Times like these I wish I could smell your the sexiness of your cologne as we embrace and share that special moment where our hearts beat as one

Times like these I wish I could see your true feelings for me because sometimes you leave me confused referencing to

where you stand as opposed to my
position

Times like these I wish I could hear you
soft whispers as we become entangled in a
web of delightful fulfilling moments that
you and I share when we do the things we
do

Times like these get harder and harder to
overcome when you're nowhere to be
found during my time of need but I do
know one thing you will appear soon.

Love kept my grandmother from forgetting me.

Memories Within

Here I sit by my favorite window in the
living room surrounded by the golden rays
of the sun.
The house is full of seemingly familiar
faces that yet I can not seem to recognize
There are young ones, old ones, round
ones, long ones and I know not one.

A petite, dark skinned woman approaches
me with years of hardship buried behind
her brown eyes

She lets her arms out like a red carpet to
welcome me into a subtle embrace

My thoughts must not hide themselves
well as proven by the confusion expressed
on my face

"Who are you?" I ask. "What are you trying to do to me?"

"Mother I'm your daughter, don't you know your own family?"

I, instead , give her a handshake because I don't take up well with strangers.

The look on her face weakened my heart. I don't think I've ever seen disappointment so vividly.

She's my daughter. How can I not know my own daughter if I am the one who bore her?

If she was my child then, as any mother I consider her my everything but if I don't know her does that mean I am left with nothing?

"James where are you? You better not be trying to push your brother off the bed again!!!"

I yelled down the hall. No reply from either of my boys just blank stares,worried stares from unfamiliar faces then one approaches and says "Grandma, James has been living in New York

for over five years now and Sammie...well he passed away last year remember?"

Remember???? What has happened to me? My memories have become memories themselves and all I can do is sit here

amongst these stranges. Strangers that
claim to be my family but

yet I know not one. Whoever these people
are I love them and I can't help it because
obviously

they are all I have left.
(In memory of Grandmother Mary Lizzie)

Sometimes, with LOVE comes heartbreak.

The Introduction

So many things left unsaid that I wanted
and needed to say
but I never got the chance to.
Every word that I held in my heart to tell
you stayed in
captivation up until the time I walked out
the door.

I barely spoke a word during the
awkwardness of
the introduction and stillness of the
silence, that
we tried to break with conversation
starters that only
resulted in nonchalant yes's and no's and
other simple
short maybes

Every word that was held in my heart to tell you stayed in
captivation and after the introduction it seems as if they've
gotten a life sentence.

I walked out the door. Too much tension for one's own
cardiovascular muscle to withstand so I, in my right
mind left, yet saddened by the fact that you never
came after me to even attempt to explain the reason
of her existence in your life...the life that was supposed only
consist of you and I...

As I sat in my car those words that were held captive in my

my heart came flowing out of my tear
ducts. With every drop of
salty solution came

"I love you more than you'd ever know."
"You're the one I dream of growing old
with."
"I love the way your arms feel when
they're wrapped around me."
"You've been on my mind since the day
you left."
"My soul dances to the beat of your
heart."

These were the words that were left
unsaid but instead
of being whispered out of my mouth in to
your ear they
rolled down the brown baby smooth skin
of my cheeks

into a handkerchief that I plan on
throwing away..........
on the day I get over you.

LOVE: Self-Inflicted Pain

Never has a guy done anything like what he has done to me.
Never has anyone ever brought out the feelings that he withdrew from me.
I feel like such a punk for feeling like this, it's against my self nature. I don't know what to do.
I don't know how to start over because all that I had of me he has put it in his back pocket and walked away.

I know I messed up but what can I do? I was a mess when he came into my life.
There are brighter days ahead I'm sure of it, til then I'm still wandering around in the dark.
The day he walked away he left a trail of the many pieces that made up the woman

that he wanted me to be so maybe just maybe
I can gather up enough of them to put her back together and they'll lead me back to him.

You never know what you had until it's gone which actually doesn't apply to me because honestly he was never mine to begin with.
(cont)
Yet I loved him.
He knew what this was before it started but I let my misdirected heart and blinded eyes lead me.

Never again will I allow this to happen....well at least not until he comes around again.

Sad isn't it?

Vs. Self

I know who I am and where I'm going vs.
"What am I gonna do with my life? Why
have I taken this path?"
I'm a beautiful voluptuous woman can't
nobody stop me vs.
"Ugh there are so many flaws no wonder
I'm alone."
I don't live to impress no man if he can't
accept me for me then to heck with him
vs.
"I gotta find my best jeans, the ones that
make my butt look good so that when I
walk his way he won't be able to keep his
eyes off of me."
I'm happy with where I am and wouldn't
trade it for anything vs.
"I really wish I was somewhere else right
about now."

I walk with my head held high like a confident woman should vs.
"I'm just searching the skies for an answer as to why my life is so out of control."
I speak with substance so that when people hear me they have no choice but to listen vs.

(cont)
"I tell so many lies I wouldn't know the truth if it walked up to me pissed on my shoe."
I love to have a good time and make others around me laugh vs.
"If only you knew what I was going through."

Toxicity and LOVE are not synonymous.

Done.

I can't love you fully the way
      I used to,

    common Sense and a shattered heart
               won't
             allow it.

Don't you dare try to sail your dreams of
      loving me again
In my direction because these tides of
doubt
      created by your lies will
         only wash you away.

I'm not the reason for me being this way
      well, maybe
I'm the one who said we could make it
work first
But you knew you no good long before we
met.

Could you not have warned me?

Minuit

I thought of you tonight
as my thoughts fell to the gravitational
pull of
seduction and lust.

To lust that arose
from the sweet valley between my thighs
searched the air with waves of desire
As I was fiending for
your touch,
your kiss,
your air.

I
Just
Simply
Desire
You.

My fingertips extend into
a familiar place as they moved
to the rhythm that was once ours.
It wasn't ours anymore.
Still, that doesn't stop me from thinking
of you.

Can't Get It Back

There's so much I want to say
to you and so much that I want
to ask

I just know that when I speak
to you, you can't answer back.

My life is different without you here
I'm becoming more guarded by the day.

Someone came into my life but he doesn't
realize he's in an uphill battle of
constantly
trying to repair a heart he didn't even
break.

I don't know how I feel right now
in this present time.
When memories of the the moments

we shared start to flash across my mind
I always hate it because I always wonder
"what if..."

It's a love hate relationship
between my heart and my brain.
(cont)
You were my true love but I know if
you were to ever come back the growth
I've had won't allow myself to love you
the same.

Complacent

I can't decide on how I feel
it's a little bit of everything
I'm where I thought I wanted to be

      Something's off tho.

I don't know what it is but it's hard to f
put a finger on exact what it is when
there's
no emotion.

LOVE can run its course just like any regular season.

Be The One

Ever been in a situation where
you have so much love to give but,
you haven't found anyone that's ready to
receive it or even reciprocate it in same
manner
they took it from you?

I want a love that's only for me like
when I'm with him no one else matters
I want him to be strong enough to not give
in to the fact
that his flesh is weak.

Nowadays it seems like that's too much to
ask.

The End

They say when you actually love someone
that feeling never really goes away
But what other possible way is there to
explain how I feel for you...correction
what I felt for you.
That lovebug is slowly but surely
retracting its deadly venom from my
brain, my heart, my soul
But what choice did it have?
We were its source of strength.
Now that there's only me left here for it to
feed off of
it will never be as strong as it once was,
that feeling will never be as strong as it
once was.

Leave it in the Past

Trust is so hard to give these days,
well at least for me.

It's the same thing, different guy telling
the same lie

Almost makes me question
if I'm even worthy of having a loving
partner.

How do I keep making the same mistake?

How do I get caught up with the same
type of guy?

How do I prevent this from happening
again?

I almost feel as if my heart isn't meant to
be given to anyone.
This isn't where I thought I would be.

Just as lost as I was when I was 18

Cursing every partner that I've ever had
that has
tainted my perception of love.

Will I end up taking it out on my partner
in the future?

No, I'm not. He doesn't deserve to be
mistreated
for my bad taste in men.

Hopeful

Someday
I won't be as guarded as
they have made me and
someday,
someone will come my way that
I can love fully

I know
I will one day.
I just hope
I don't mess it up.

To The Men I Loved

I loved you all at one point, in some form
or fashion.
Yeah maybe a couple bonds were stronger
than others but yet ...I loved you.

One- You were loved truly, madly loved.
Your chest was the abyss all of my worries
melted into.
I loved you before I met you.
I loved you even more after we met.
However,
over time we realized that we were much
better as friends.

Two- We worked. We actually did, until
we didn't.
There's a saying that the one who cares
the least

is the one that controls the relationship. I gotta say, dear, you were definitely in control.
I would give you my last but I came to the realization that
to you...I was last.
The love I had for you was like none other. The hurt I experienced from you was like no other.

Three- If anyone ever believed in being in the right place, at the wrong time.
That's us, that's this. We matched so well but we knew we couldn't be. You were more than a lover, you were what I always thought was my safest place in the world.

The loves of my past have taught me so much about who I am that I can only be thankful for them

LOVE is our superpower,
don't abuse it.

Don't Take No Wooden Nickels

Finding yourself is probably one of the
greatest accomplishments you could ever
have
There's something so freeing about
having your own identity and not having
your identity buried in a person, a
relationship, or work
When you love yourself the right way, you
shouldn't allow anyone to treat you any
less than what you know you deserve

I can say that I have found myself and
there is no question that I love the hell out
of me.
My grandmother always used to say
"don't take no wooden nickels"
I think she'd be proud of the woman I've
become

Repaired

Well I can say I did it now.
The taste of your name is no longer bitter,
nor am I bitter in any sense of the
meaning.

I have freed myself of you and your ill-
fated grip.
Left with a sound mind and still a loving
heart I am no longer bound to you

You thought you broke me, honestly I
thought you did too but through prayer,
meditation, and spending more time with
self care I can say that I've repaired
myself, my heart, and am open to love
again

My Love is Everlasting

We've had our struggles and our strong points as time was slowly passing

One thing's for sure just as the clear spring water is pure, my love is everlasting.

Our trust in one another is our umbrella as lies became the drowning rain.

There is no limit to how far you would go for me and I for you , we've withstood a great deal of pain

We are never afraid to share any of our dreams, concerns, or even our greatest fears.

We share the same sense of humor, so we act like kids and let laughter cast out our tears

Although the time we spend together has our days surely passing, one thing's for sure King, my love is everlasting.

My Everything

You have given me a brand new
understanding of the meaning of love
For it was you that showed me that I can
do anything, if and only if, I believe in
myself.
You are my guide to finding a new place of
happiness through all of my sadness

You are the joy that true love is to bound
to bring
You are my one and only, my light in the
dark, my everything

LOVE is the support you've shown reading this book.

I thank you tremendously.

About the Author

Krystal was raised in a small town of Barnesville, Georgia. She is a mother, hard worker, and poet. When she is not attending her son's sport events or working she can be found hiking, writing, or travelling.

Krystal has been writing poetry since she was in elementary school however, it was much later when she realized her talent. After reading a poem she wrote for their anniversary titled "A Once in a Lifetime chance, her parents pushed her to take her writing more seriously. She kept writing and journaling to help her work on her craft. *Aglaonema* is a small collection of some of her work and an introduction to Krystal as an author.

Made in the USA
Columbia, SC
02 February 2021

32072961R00043